Curriculum Visions

Spelling Book 1

Sarah Lindsay

Curriculum Visions

Spelling

Teacher's Resource Book
There is a Teacher's Resource Book to accompany this Pupil Book.

Dedicated Web Site
There's more information about other great Curriculum Visions resources and a wealth of supporting material available at:
www.CurriculumVisions.com

Author
Sarah Lindsay

Art Director
Duncan McCrae

Senior Designer
Adele Humphries

Editors
Robert Anderson and Gillian Gatehouse

Illustrations
David Woodroffe

Designed and produced by
EARTHSCAPE EDITIONS

Printed in China by
WKT Company Ltd

This product is manufactured from sustainable managed forests. For every tree cut down at least one more is planted.

First published in 2006 by
Atlantic Europe Publishing Company Ltd
Reprinted June 2006

Curriculum Visions Spelling Book 1
A CIP record for this book is available from the British Library.

ISBN-10: 1-86214-510-5
ISBN-13: 978-1-86214-510-8

Contents

Unit 1

a

dad	fan	cat	band
pad	man	hat	hand
sad	pan	mat	sand

Making words

Finish the labels for the picture.

Can you find one more **a** word in the picture? Write the word.

Using words

Use the words to help you write the sentences.

bag tap ham Pam rat rag bat cap

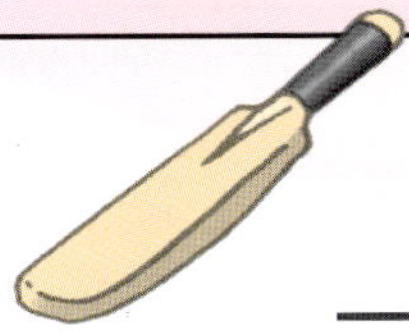

1 **cat** rhymes with ________ and ________.

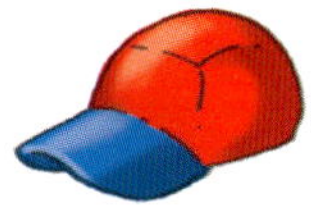

2 **map** rhymes with ________ and ________.

3 **jam** rhymes with ________ and ________.

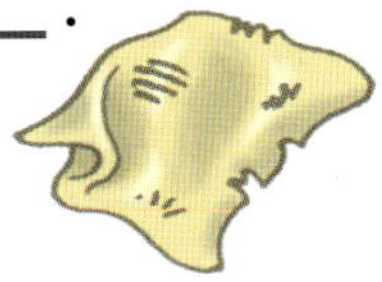

4 **tag** rhymes with ________ and ________.

Puzzle corner

Look at the first letter of each of the words.
Write the words in the order the first letters come in the alphabet.

dog bat ant egg cat

This is called putting the words in **alphabetical order.**

Unit 2

e

bed	beg	hen	bent
fed	peg	men	sent
red	leg	ten	tent

Making words

Write an e word to match each picture.

1

r_d

2

t_n

3

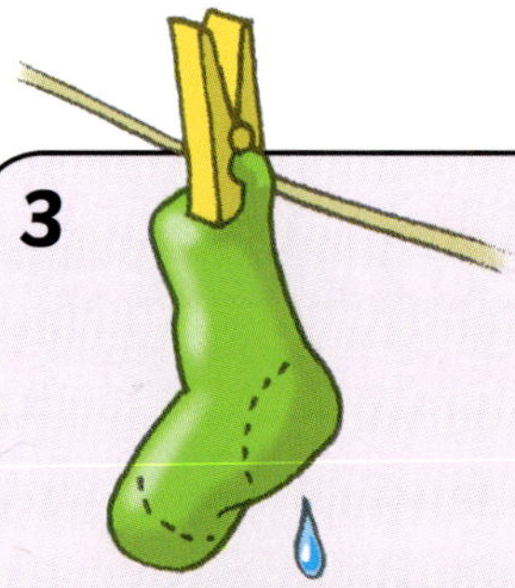

p_g

4

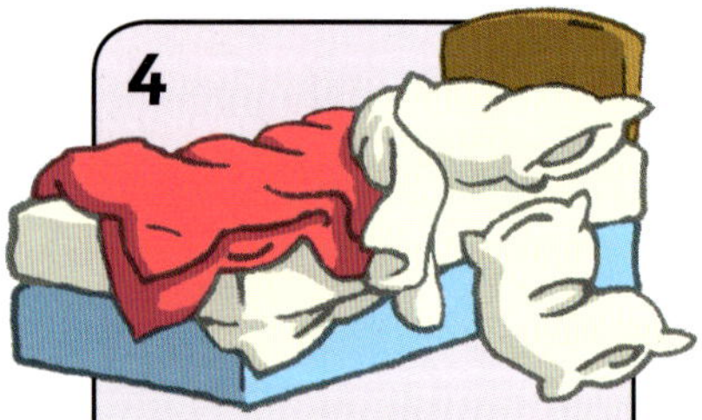

b_d

5

b_g

6

m_n

Draw a picture of a new e word.

Using words

Lots of words rhyme with **pet**.
List all the words you can think of.

Puzzle corner

Match the labels to the pictures.

- paper
- books
- pencils
- coats
- sink
- paint

Unit 3

i

big	bin	hit	hill
dig	fin	pit	mill
pig	pin	sit	pill

Making words

Finish the labels for the picture.

Can you find one more **i** word in the picture? Write the word.

Using words

Copy the words in rhyming families.

tin	did	hip

zip bin mix

din dip win

pip hid lid

One **i** word does not fit into a rhyming family.
Which word is it?

Puzzle corner

Write a short story.
It must have each of these words in it.
Underline these words in your story.

look play away going said

Draw a picture to go with your story.

Unit 4

o

dog	hop	cod	lock
fog	mop	nod	rock
log	top	rod	sock

Making words

Write an o word to match each picture.

1
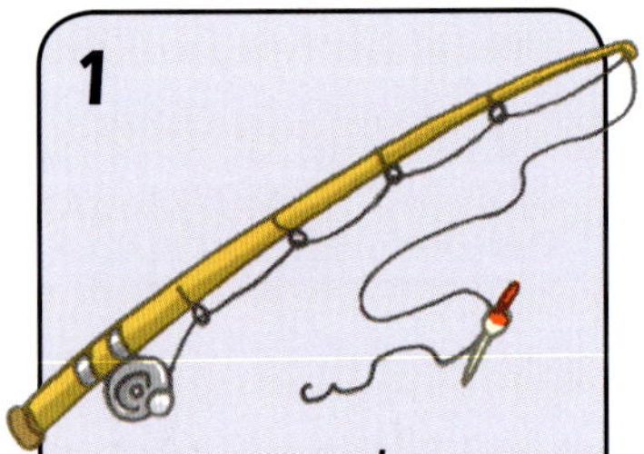
r_d

2

f_g

3

h_p

4

m_p

5

l_g

6

d_g

Draw a picture of a new o word.

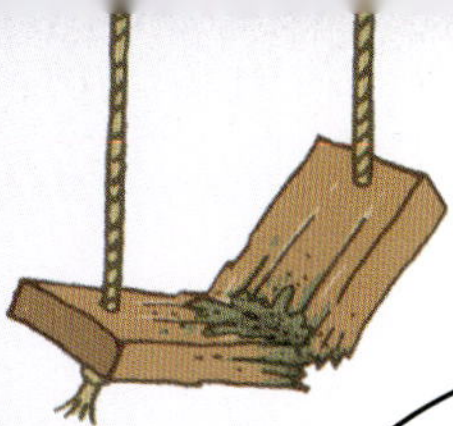

Using words

Lots of words rhyme with **cot**.
List all the words you can find.

Can you find a word that rhymes with **box**?

Puzzle corner

Copy the words. Draw a line between the words which have the same spelling pattern.

1 tent	duck
2 land	mill
3 rock	band
4 hill	sent
5 luck	sock

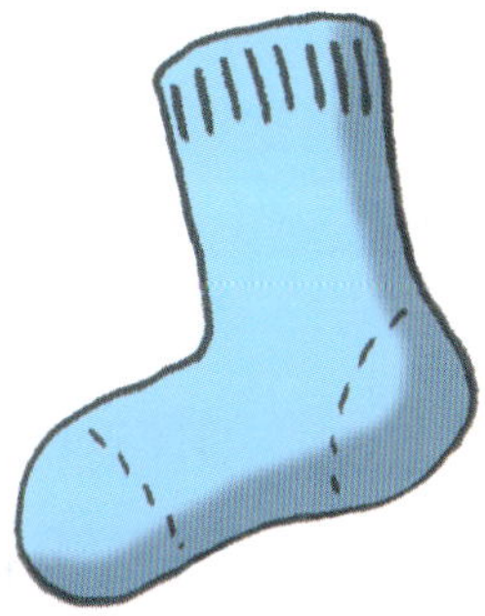

Unit 5

u

up	fun	bug	duck
cup	run	jug	luck
pup	sun	rug	suck

Making words

Finish the labels for the picture.

Can you find one more picture of a **u** word? Write the word.

Using words

Use the words to help you write the sentences.

bun sum cub mum run hut tub nut

1 **sun** rhymes with  ________ and ________ 

2 **hum** rhymes with 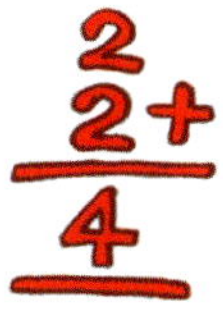

________ and ________ 

3 **rub** rhymes with  ________ and ________ 

4 **cut** rhymes with  ________ and ________ 

Puzzle corner

abcdefghijklmnopqrstuvwxyz

Put these words in alphabetical order.

jug hut tub rug sum bug

Unit 6
sh

fish

shop

splash

shed	fish	shelf	brush
ship	wish	shell	flash
shop	rush	shock	splash

Making words

Write a **sh** word to match each picture.

1

___ip

2

___ed

3

___ell

4

___elf

5

___op

6

___ock

Choose two **sh** words and draw them in a picture.
Write the **sh** words on your picture.

Using words

Write the **sh** words you can see in the picture.

How many **sh** words did you find?

Puzzle corner

Copy these words.
Each word has a shorter word in it.
Draw a line under the short word.

1 shot	**2** shop	**3** sham
4 dash	**5** smash	**6** crush

Write two more words that have a short word in them.

Unit 7
ch

chin	chest	catch	scratch
chip	chick	lunch	stitch
chop	chimp	pinch	switch

Making words

Add **ch** to each of the letters to make a word.

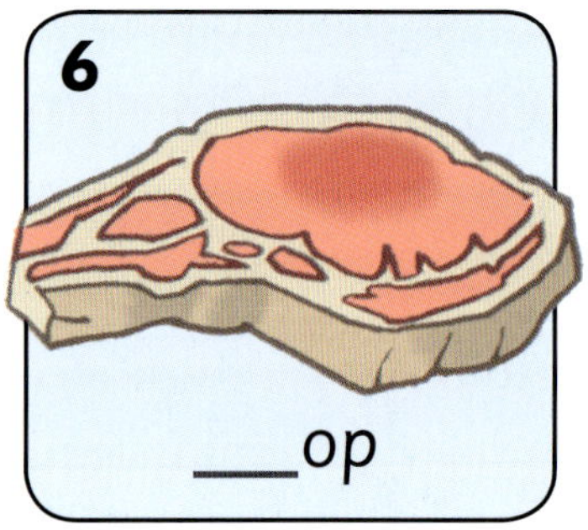

Draw a picture of a word beginning with **ch**.
Write the word on your picture.

Using words

Add **ch** to the beginning or end of these letters to make a word.

est

it

snat

ick

swit

mun

Write a sentence.
Use two of the words you have made.

Puzzle corner

What colour?

1 A colour with the same name as a fruit.
2 The colour of grass.
3 The colour of a field after it has snowed.
4 A letterbox is this colour.
5 The colour of a pig after it has rolled in mud!
6 This colour rhymes with bellow.

orange **white** **red** **brown** **green** **yellow**

Unit 8

th

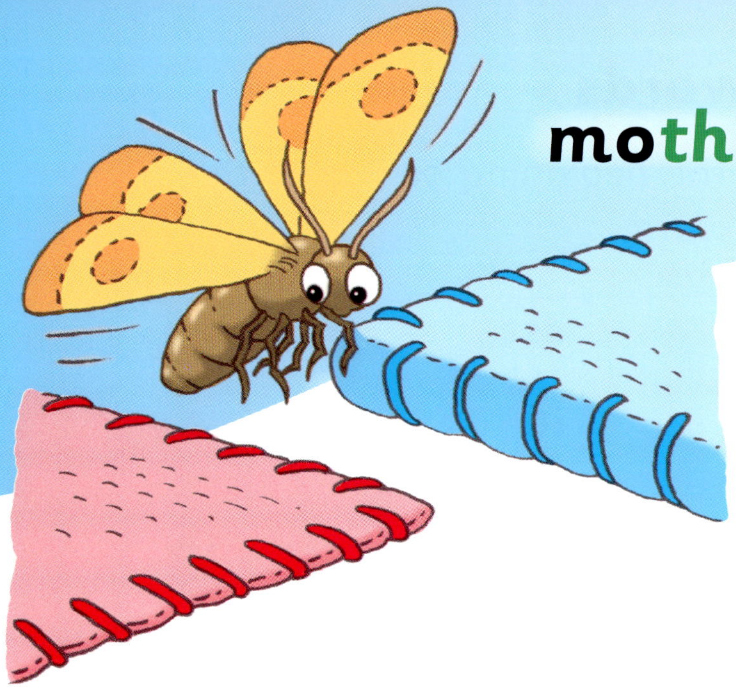

the	that	cloth	thing
then	thin	moth	thick
this	them	width	think

Making words

Finish the word sums.

1 th + is = ________

2 th + ____ = them

3 th + ink = ________

4 th + ____ = then

5 th + ing = ________

6 th + ____ = that

Using words

Fill the gap in each sentence with a **th** word.

thick	**This**	**teeth**	**fifth**	**They**

1 ________ is my book.

2 It is the ________ of March.

3 ________ all woke up and had breakfast.

4 Aimee cleaned her ________ .

5 Kyle has a ________, warm coat.

Write two sentences, each with a **th** word.

Puzzle corner

Copy the table.
Sort the words into the topics.

Islands	Food	Books

treasure **words** **reading** **supermarket** **palm tree** **lunch** **sea** **sand** **cooking** **dictionary** **vegetables** **fairytale**

Unit 9
ll

ill	bell	ball	drill
hill	well	doll	spell
mill	yell	gull	smell

Making words

Match each picture with its ll word.

mill   doll   hill   bell   yell   gull

1

2

3

4

5

6

Write a sentence using a ll word.

Using words

Add **all** or **ell** to each of the letters to make a word.

How many words can you make?

b		**all**
f		
h	**+**	
s		**ell**
w		

Puzzle corner

Finish the short story. Use the words.

they He you was said

Daniel ________ bored.

________ had to wait for his sister.

"Are ________ coming?" he asked.

"Yes I am!" she ________ .

At last ________ were on their way home!

Unit 10

ff
ss

cuff	hiss	mess	cliff
puff	kiss	dress	stiff
stuff	miss	press	sniff

Making words

Add **ff** or **ss** to match each word with the picture.

1

ki___

2

me___

3

pu___

4

hi___

5

dre___

6

cu___

Draw a picture for a **ff** or **ss** word.

Using words

Copy the words you can find in the picture.

fluff	cross
dress	cuff
sniff	moss
hiss	toss
puff	press

Puzzle corner

Where in the classroom would you find the clues? Match the clue to the right answer.

1	Where reading books are found.	**carpet**
2	Where you use a mouse!	**painting area**
3	Where it can get messy.	**reading corner**
4	Where you sit and listen quietly.	**computer table**

Unit 11

ng

king	bang	long	hung
ring	fang	pong	lung
wing	hang	song	sung

Making words

Write a **ng** word to match each picture.

1

wi___

2
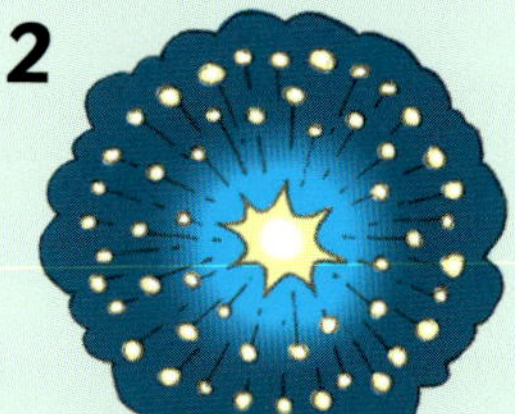
ba___

3

ri___

4
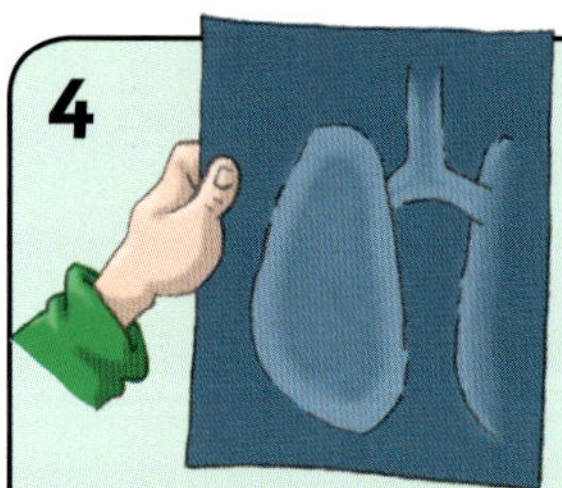
lu___

5

ki___

6

fa___

Write a **ng** word in a funny sentence.

Using words

Copy the table. Sort the **ng** words into rhyming families.

ang	**ing**	**ong**	**ung**

long

hang

gong

gang

rung

sing

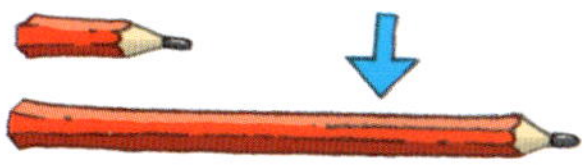

dung

ring

Puzzle corner

Copy this diary page.
Fill it in with something you are doing on each day.

Monday ______________________________

Tuesday ______________________________

Wednesday ______________________________

Thursday ______________________________

Friday ______________________________

Saturday ______________________________

Sunday ______________________________

Unit 12

cl
fl
sl

clap	flag	slim	clock
clip	flan	slip	flock
club	flat	slug	slick

Making words

Draw a picture for each word.
Write the word next to each picture.

1 *flag*
2 clip
3 slug
4 *flan*

Choose a **cl**, **fl** and **sl** word.
Write them all in one sentence.

Using words

How many words can you make?

cl	+	ap
fl		an
sl		at
		ip
		ot

Puzzle corner

Can you find a hidden word in each of these words? Write the word you have found.

1 flap　**2** plot　**3** block
4 cluck　**5** slid　**6** click

Write two more words that have a short word in them.

Unit 13

dr
gr
tr

drag	gran	tram	drink
drip	grin	trap	grill
drum	grip	trip	track

Making words

Draw a picture for each word.
Write the word next to each picture.

1 drip
2 grin
3 trap
4 drum

Choose a **dr**, **gr** and **tr** word.
Write them all in one sentence.

Using words

How many words can you make?

dr	+	ab
		an
gr		im
		ip
tr		ill

Puzzle corner

Find five **dr**, **gr** or **tr** words in the wordsearch.

d	r	i	p	t
f	t	o	p	r
g	r	a	n	i
s	a	u	m	c
r	p	i	l	k
a	d	r	u	m

Now add an 's' to each word to make it plural.

Unit 14

nd

band	find	bend	pound
hand	kind	send	sound
sand	mind	spend	round

Making words

Write a **nd** word to match each picture.

Remember the words in the word list will help you.

1

s_____

2

k_____

3

s_____

4

b_____

5

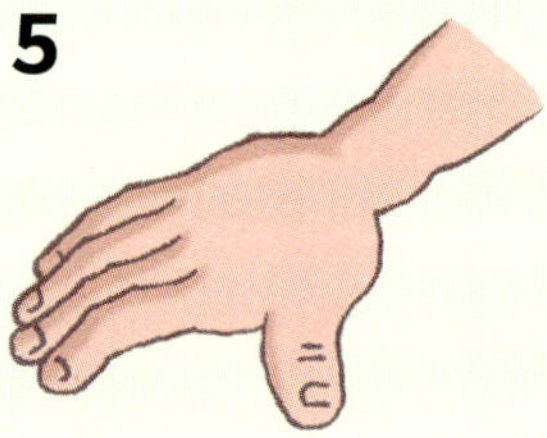

h_____

6

sp_____

Draw and label a picture for the word **bend**.

Using words

Use the words to help you write the sentences.

spend	**land**	**kind**	**found**	**pond**	**wind**

1 **hand** rhymes with ____________

2 **bond** rhymes with ____________

3 **blend** rhymes with ____________

4 **mound** rhymes with ____________

5 **find** rhymes with ____________

Puzzle corner

Look at these things that happen at school.
Write three things about each one.

Playtime	Assembly	Home time
	listening	

Unit 15

st
sp

step	nest	spot	stamp
stem	mist	spell	stand
stop	dust	spill	sting

Making words

Write **st** or **sp** at the beginning of each word.

1

___em

2

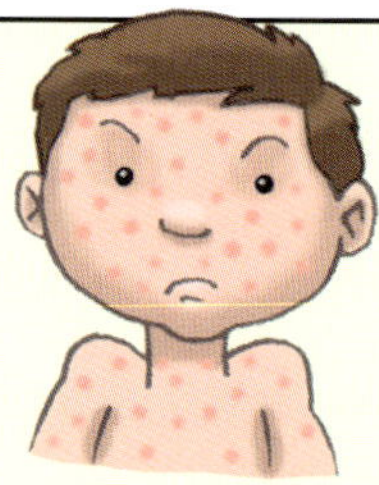

___ot

3

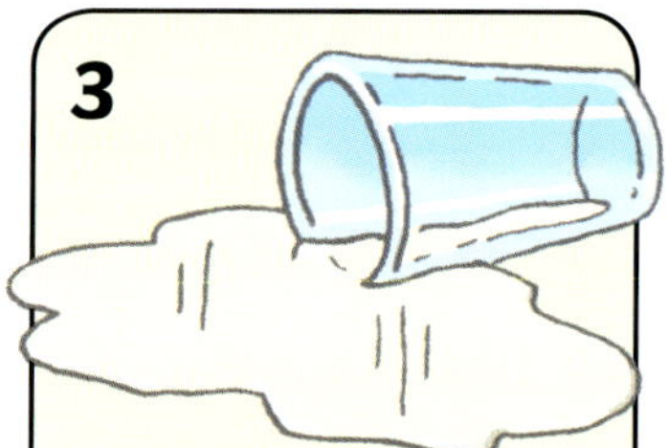

___ill

4

___op

5

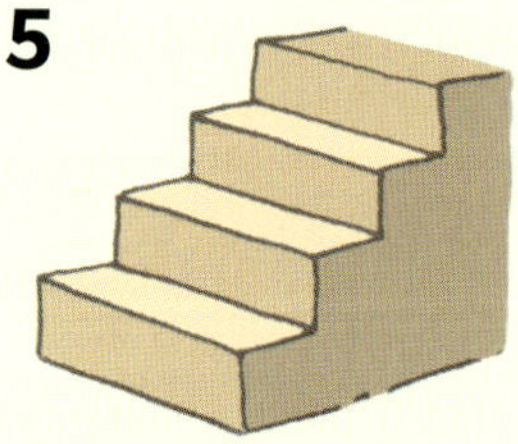

___ep

6

___amp

Draw a picture of a **st** or **sp** word.

Using words

Sort the balloons into words that rhyme.

Can you add one more word to each rhyming pair?

Puzzle corner

Write a short story.
It must have each of these words in it.
Underline these words in your story.

after castle they have said

Draw a picture to go with your story.

Unit 16
str

strap	stray	strain	stream
straw	street	strict	stretch
strip	string	strong	stripe

Making words

Match the word with the picture.

string   strong   straw   stream

1

2

3

4

Using words

How many **str** words can you find in the picture?

Write the **str** words you have found.

Puzzle corner

Copy the story. Fill in the missing verbs.

stretched	**watched**
strained	**walked**

Miss Hutt __________ her class to the hall.
It was their PE lesson. First they __________,
then they ran on the spot. Poor Kate __________
a muscle in her foot.
She __________ the rest
of the PE lesson!

Unit 17
nk

ink	bank	link	blink
pink	sank	wink	drink
sink	tank	junk	stink

Making words

Write a **nk** word to match each picture.

1

2
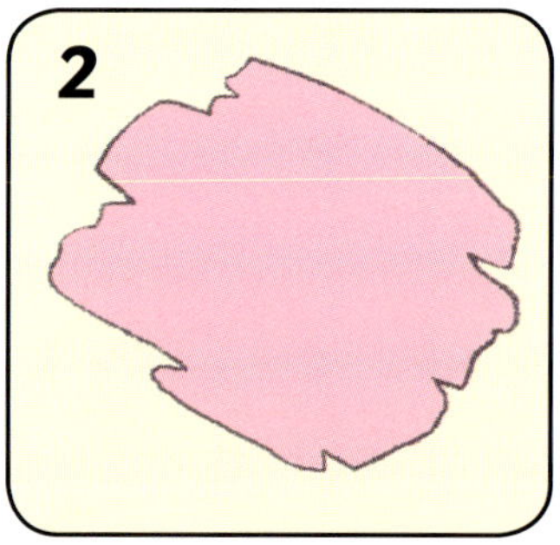

3

4

5

6
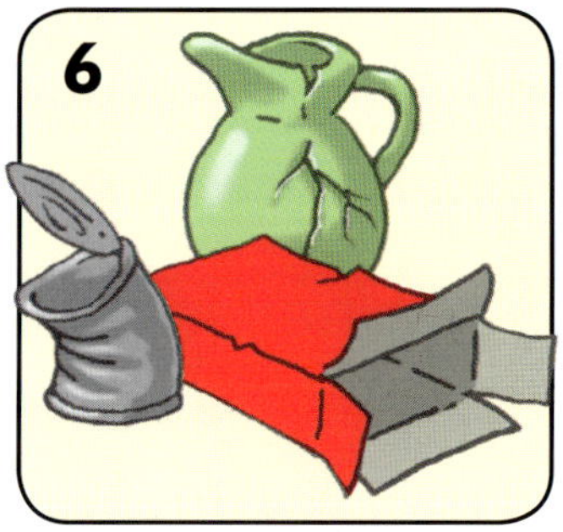

Write two sentences each with a **nk** word.

Using words

Fill in the gaps.

1 **bunk**  rhymes with ________

2 **link**  rhymes with ________

3 **stink**  rhymes with ________

4 **sank**  rhymes with ________

5 **pink**  rhymes with ________

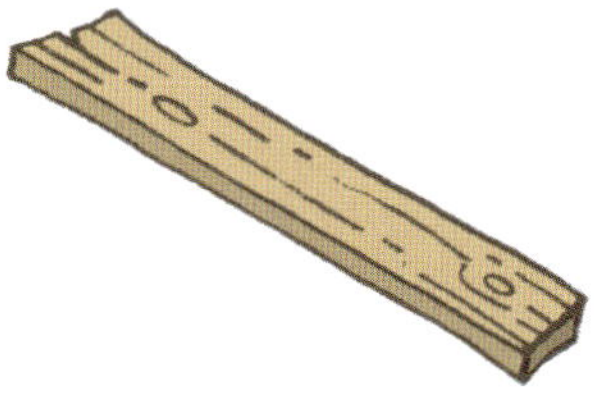

Puzzle corner

There are five vowel letters.

Fill in the table with three-lettered words.

Time yourself.

words with **a**	pad				
words with **e**	pen				
words with **i**	tin				
words with **o**	fox				
words with **u**	bus				

How long did it take you?

Unit 18

ee

bee	feed	creep	sheet
see	seed	sheep	sleet
tree	weed	sleep	sweet

Making words

Finish the labels for the picture.

Can you find one more **ee** word in the picture? Write the word.

Using words

Sort the words on the flags into rhyming families.

een **eep** **eel**

One **ee** word does not fit into the rhyming families.
Which word is it?

Puzzle corner

Match the months to the pictures.

October **December** **April** **July**

Choose two more months.
Write a sentence about something that happens in each month.

Unit 19
ai

rain

tail

aid	nail	main	frail
maid	sail	pain	snail
paid	tail	rain	trail

Making words

Write an **ai** word to match each picture.

1

s_____

2

p_____

3

m_____

4

n_____

5

r_____

6

t_____

Choose two **ai** words and write them in a sentence.

Using words

How many words can you make?

m		**aid**
p		
r	**+**	**ail**
l		
f		**ain**

Puzzle corner

Copy these words. Draw a line between the words which have the same spelling pattern.

1 **fool**	glum
2 **chimp**	dull
3 **shop**	stop
4 **gull**	shrimp
5 **drum**	tool

Unit 20

ie
i–e

lie	bike	hide	drive
pie	hike	ride	glide
tie	like	side	shine

Making words

Write an **ie** or **i–e** word to match each picture.

1

t____

2

h____

3

r____

4

b____

5

p____

6

s____

Say the words **tie** and **ride** out loud. Can you hear the same sound that the **i** makes in both words?

Using words

Fill the gap in each sentence with a word from the box.

like **drive** **lie** **hide** **tie**

1 I like to pretend to ________ a car.
2 I always ________ my sweets from my sister.
3 I can ________ my own laces.
4 I ________ on my bed.
5 I ________ to wear a scarf when it is cold.

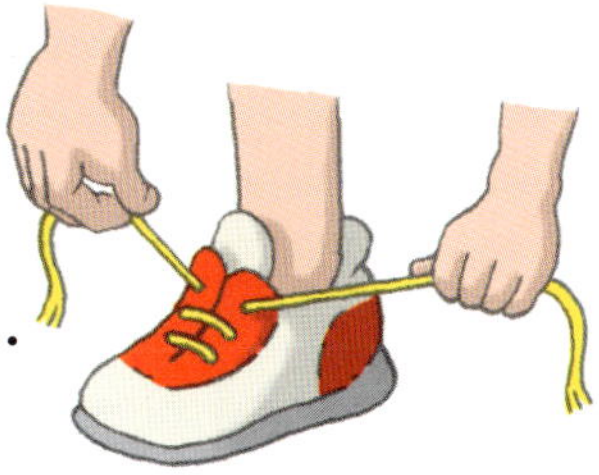

Write two sentences, each with a word from the word list.

Puzzle corner

Write your first name.
Circle all the consonant letters in it.
How many consonant letters does it have?

Now write four of your friends' names.
Circle all the consonant letters in each one.
How many consonant letters does each name have?

Who has the most consonant letters in their name?

Unit 21

oa

coat

toad

load	coal	boat	coast
road	foal	coat	roast
toad	goal	float	toast

Making words

Write an **oa** word to match each picture.

1

r____

2

g____

3

c____

4

b____

5

f____

6

t____

Choose two **oa** words and write them in a sentence.

Like this... A brown **toad** walked up a busy **road**!

Using words

Write two more words to rhyme with each word.

float croak road cloak
throat shoal toad foal

goat		
load		
goal		
soak	croak	

Puzzle corner

Find the **oa** words in the wordsearch.

z	m	t	n	l	b
t	**o**	**a**	s	t	**o**
r	**a**	i	o	h	**a**
f	n	y	w	a	s
k	f	l	**o**	**a**	t
g	r	**o**	**a**	n	h

Now add **ing** to each word you have found.

Unit 22

oo

boot	fool	moon	bloom
hoot	pool	soon	broom
root	tool	spoon	groom

Making words

Finish the labels for the picture.

Can you find one more **oo** word in the picture? Write the word.

A little help... It is used to sweep away rubbish!

Using words

Sort the words on the flags into rhyming families.

oom **oot** **oop**

One **oo** word does not fit into the rhyming families.
Which word is it?

Puzzle corner

Find the number!
Write the word of the number.

1. The number of legs a spider has.
2. The number of months in a year.
3. One taken away from twenty.
4. How old you are.
5. The number of letters in the word **banana**.

nine ten six three one twenty eight nineteen four fourteen seventeen twelve eighteen seven two five thirteen eleven fifteen sixteen

Spelling Challenge

1 sh
2 ch
3 th
4 ll
5 ss
6 ff
7 ng
8 cl
9 fl
10 sl
11 dr
12 gr
13 tr
14 nd
15 st
16 sp
17 str
18 nk
19 ee
20 ai
21 ie
22 oa
23 oo